WELCOME TO

THE GREAT BRITISH BAKE OFF COLOURING BOOK

Baking itself is relaxing but you don't need to be an expert in the kitchen to relax by colouring in (or even adding to) the illustrations in this book. And there's no reason to worry about burnt cakes or soggy bottoms when you focus exclusively on decorating!

This book celebrates all that we love about Bake Off and that includes the tent, the meadow, and British summer. As well as beautiful bread sculptures, tiered cheesecakes, Black Forest gateaux, baked Alaskas and biscuit towers, you can decorate entire batches of buns and éclairs as the Bakers do on the show.

At the back of this book you'll find an index of which bakes from the TV series inspired official Bake Off illustrator, Tom Hovey. You may well recognise a lion, a dragon, the Moulin Rouge and other favourite bakes from the show.

On your marks... get set... colour in!

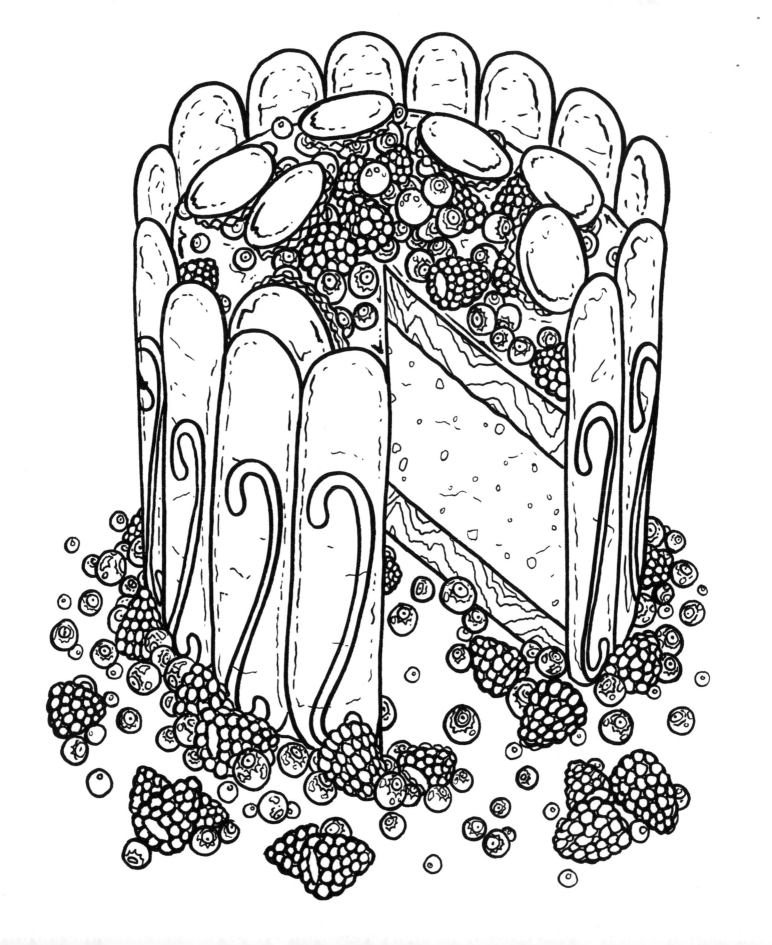

THE GREAT BRITISH
BAKE OFF
COLOURING BOOK

with illustrations by The Great British Bake Off illustrator

TOM HOVEY

HODDER &
STOUGHTON

Tom Hovey is a Welsh illustrator who lives in Bristol with his wife, Candy. He began working on the newly commissioned BBC television series *The Great British Bake Off* back in 2010, unaware that the series and his illustrations would be watched and loved by millions. Tom has drawn more than 1500 bakes for the Bake Off series as well as commissions for Channel 4, The Glastonbury Festival and Visit England.

First published in Great Britain in 2016 by Hodder & Stoughton
An Hachette UK company

4

A CIP catalogue record for this title is available from the British Library

Hardback ISBN 978 1 473 61562 5

Printed and bound in Italy by Graphicom srl

Hodder & Stoughton policy is to use papers that are natural, renewable and recyclable products and made from wood grown in sustainable forests. The logging and manufacturing processes are expected to conform to the environmental regulations of the country of origin.

Hodder & Stoughton Ltd
Carmelite House
50 Victoria Embankment
London EC4Y 0DZ

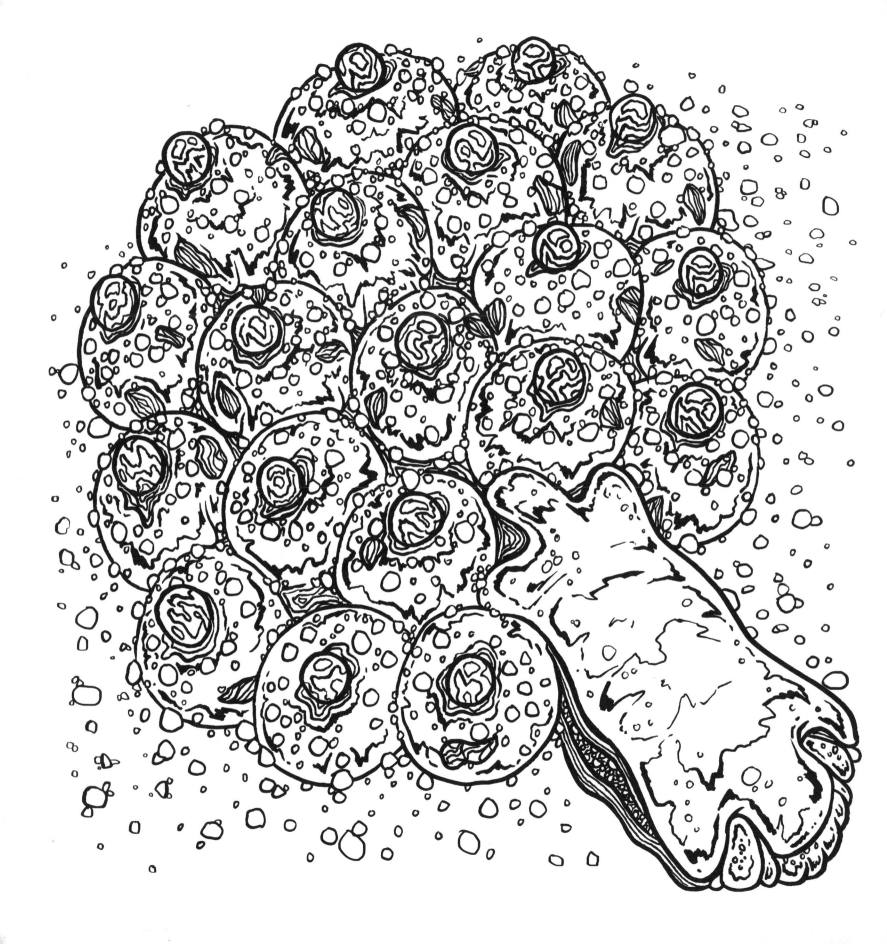

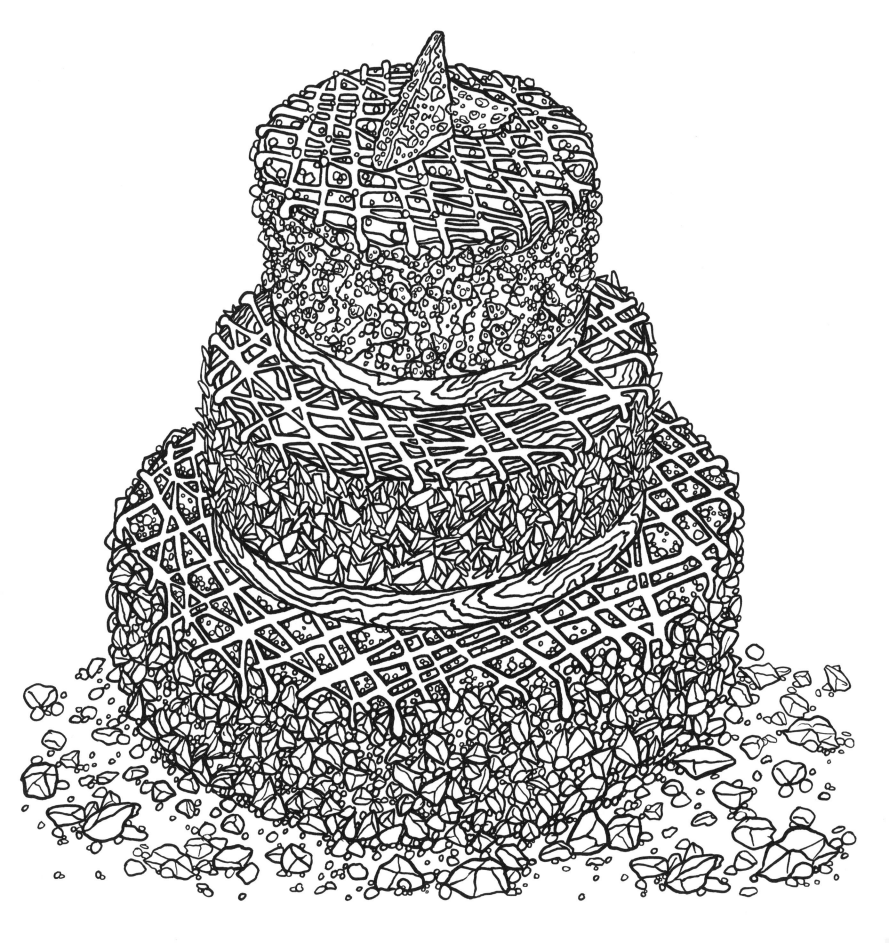

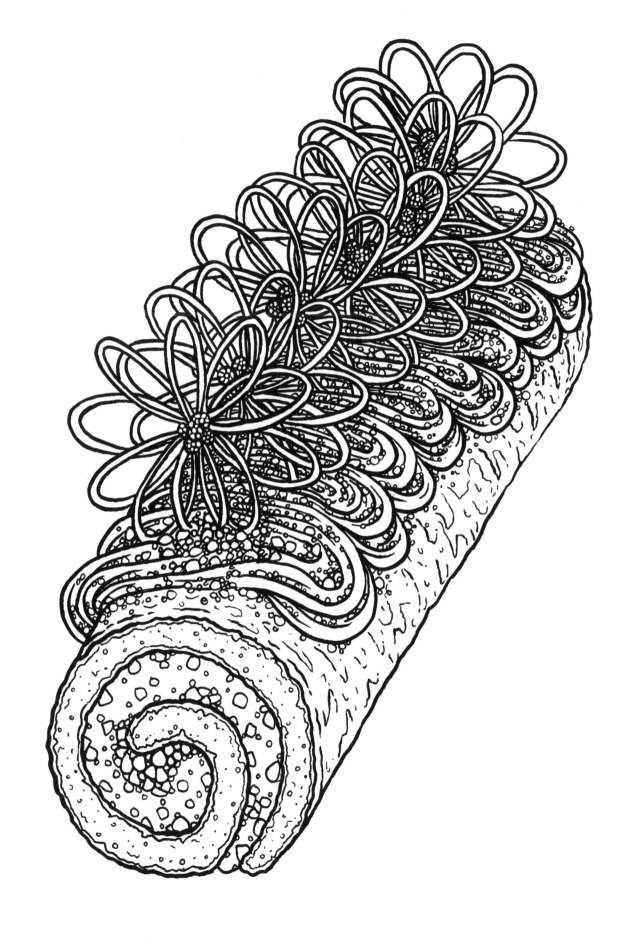

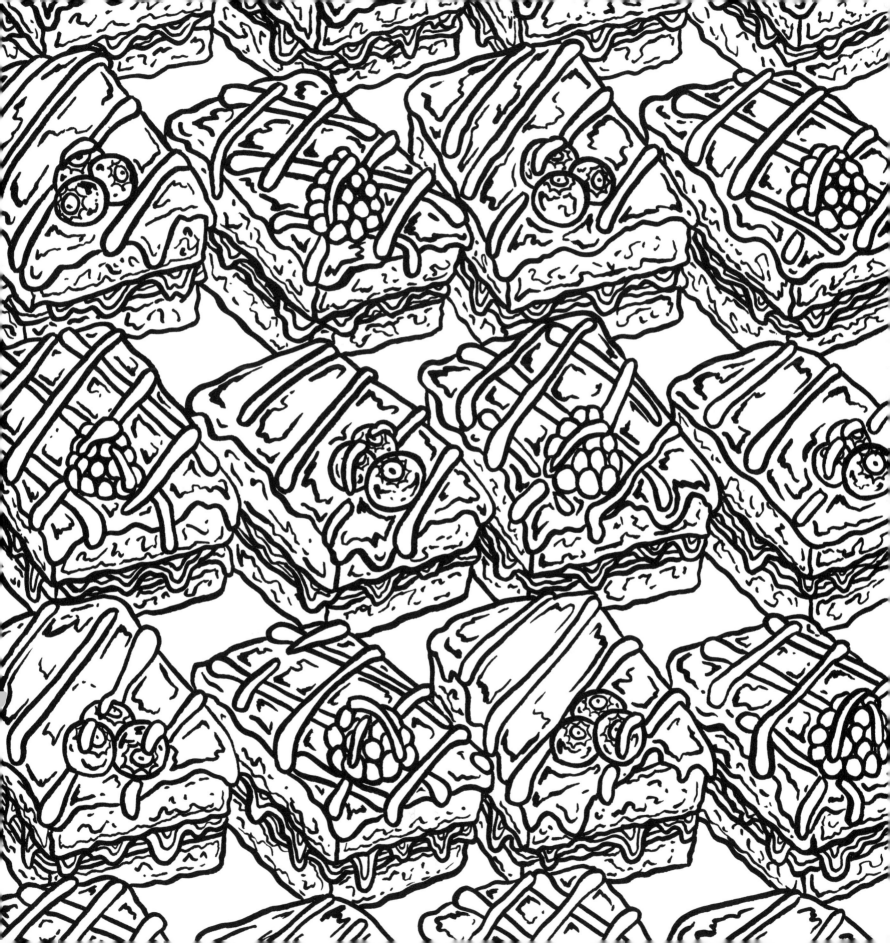

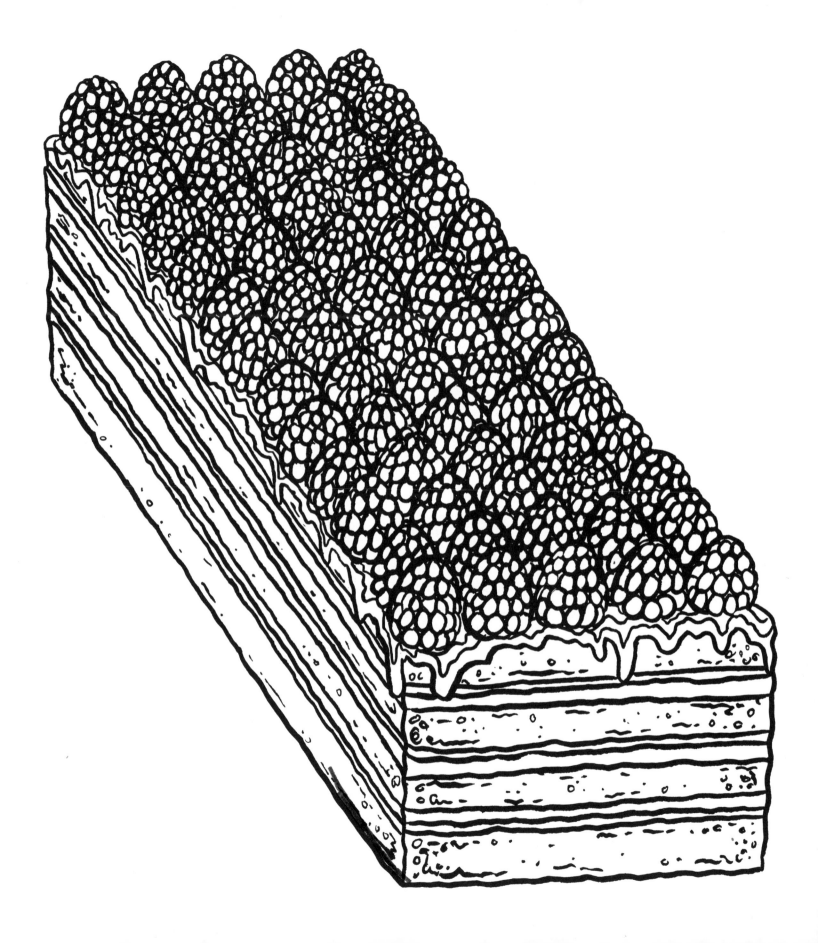

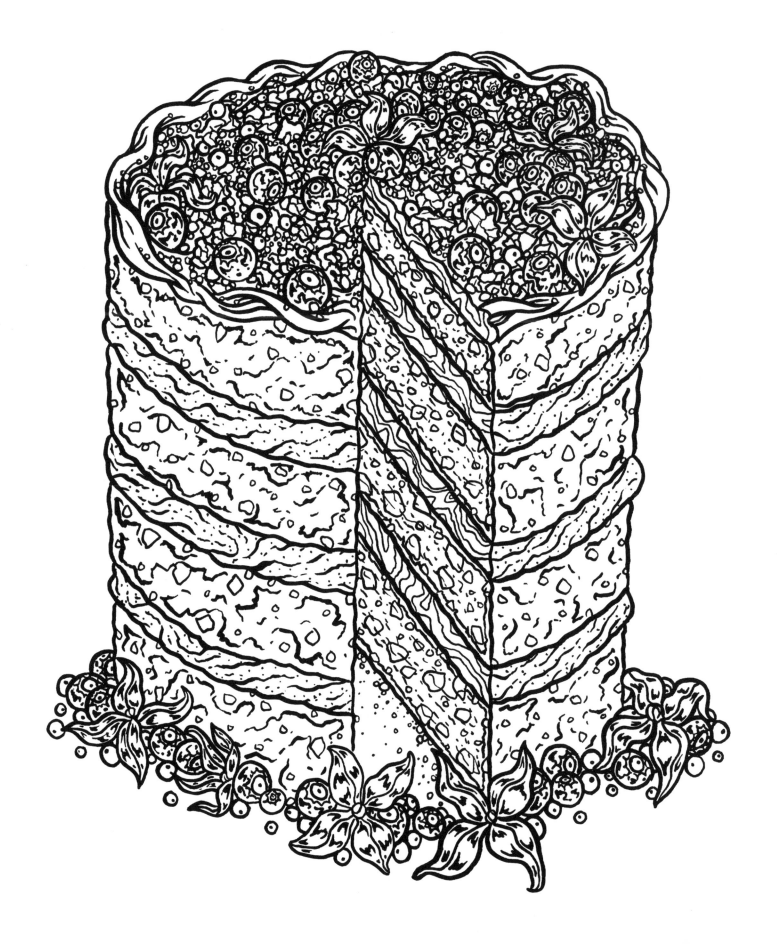

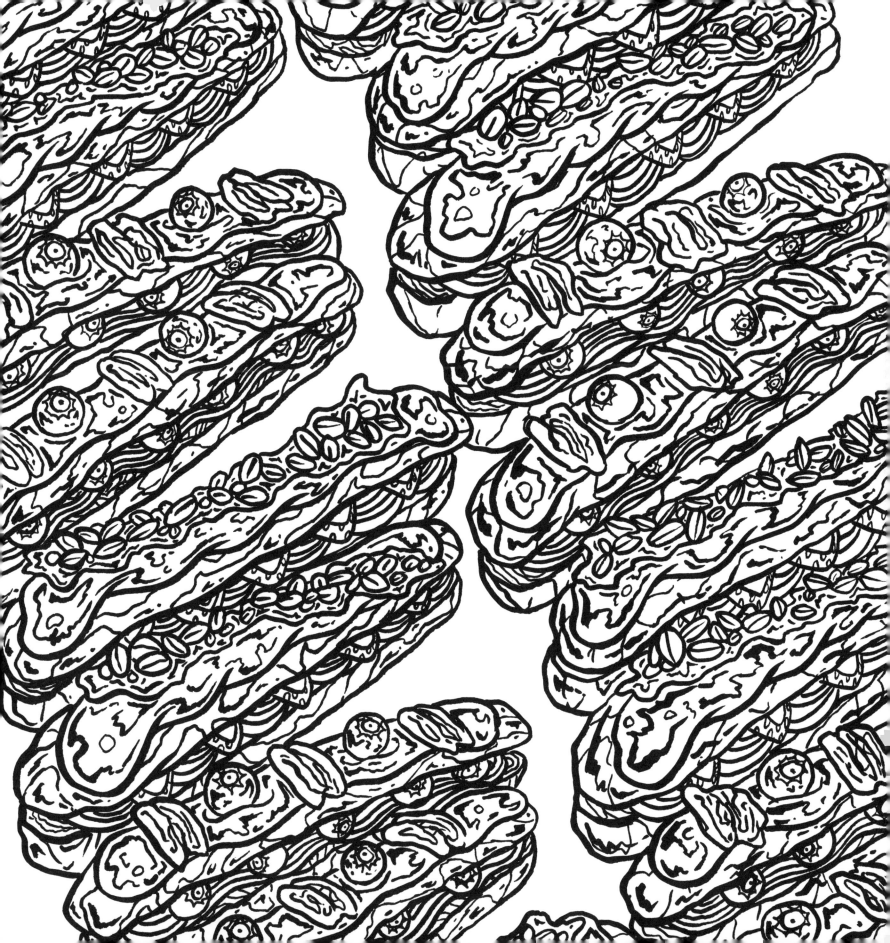

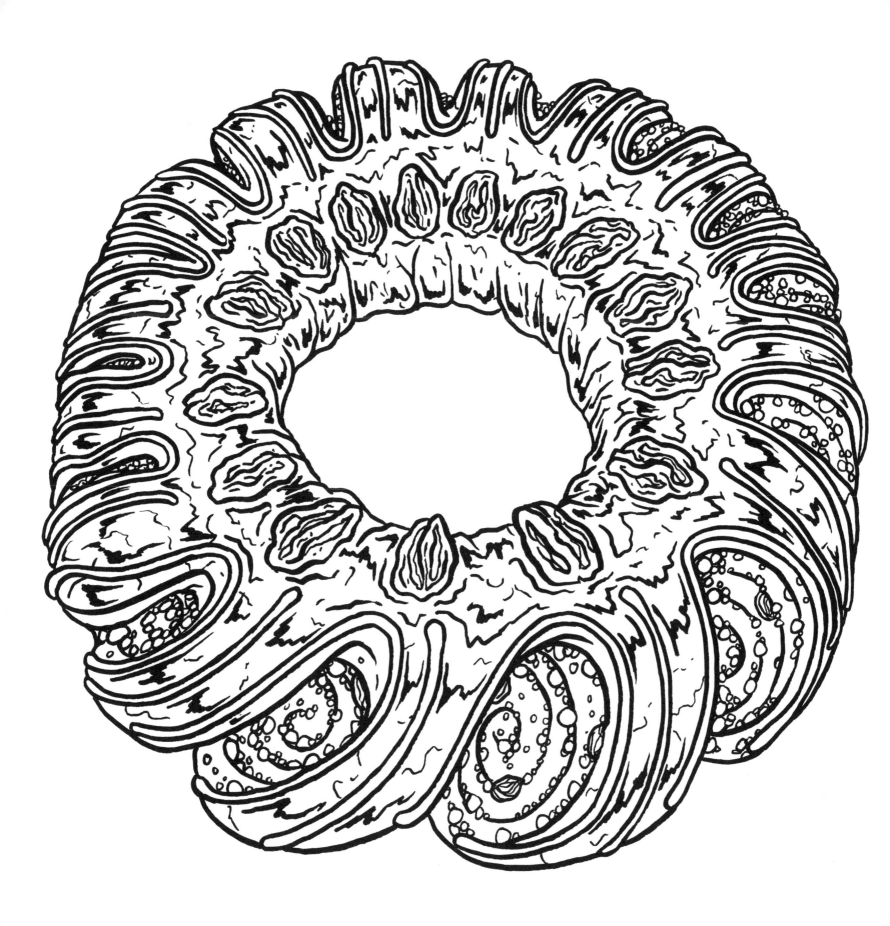

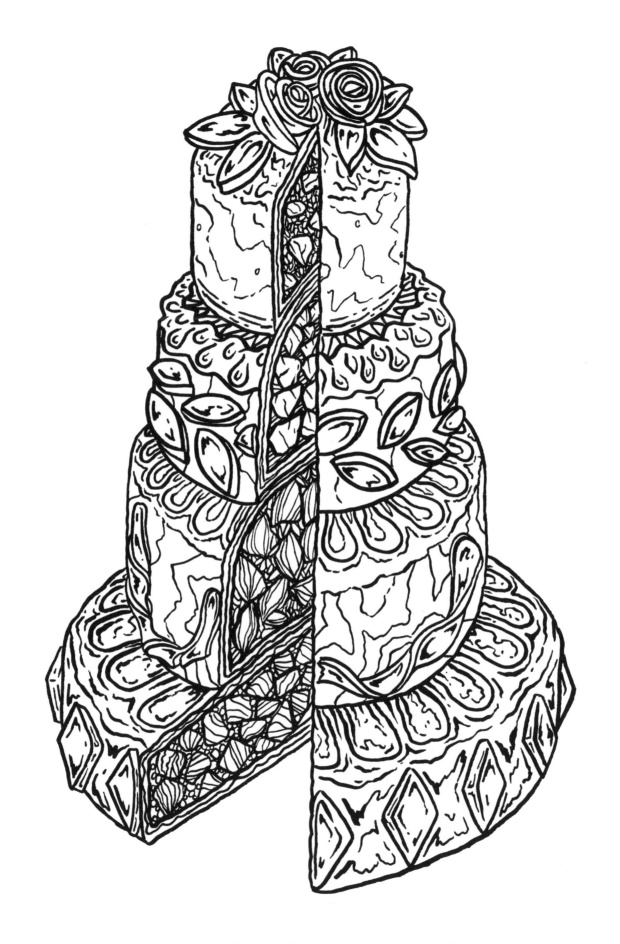

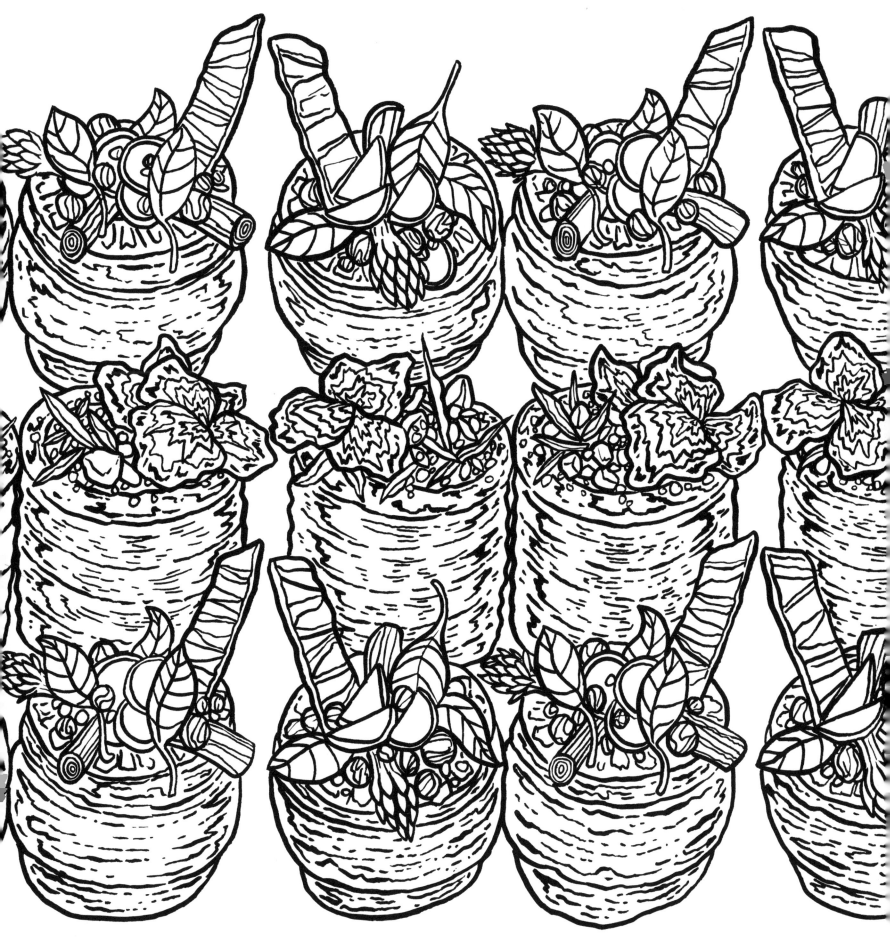

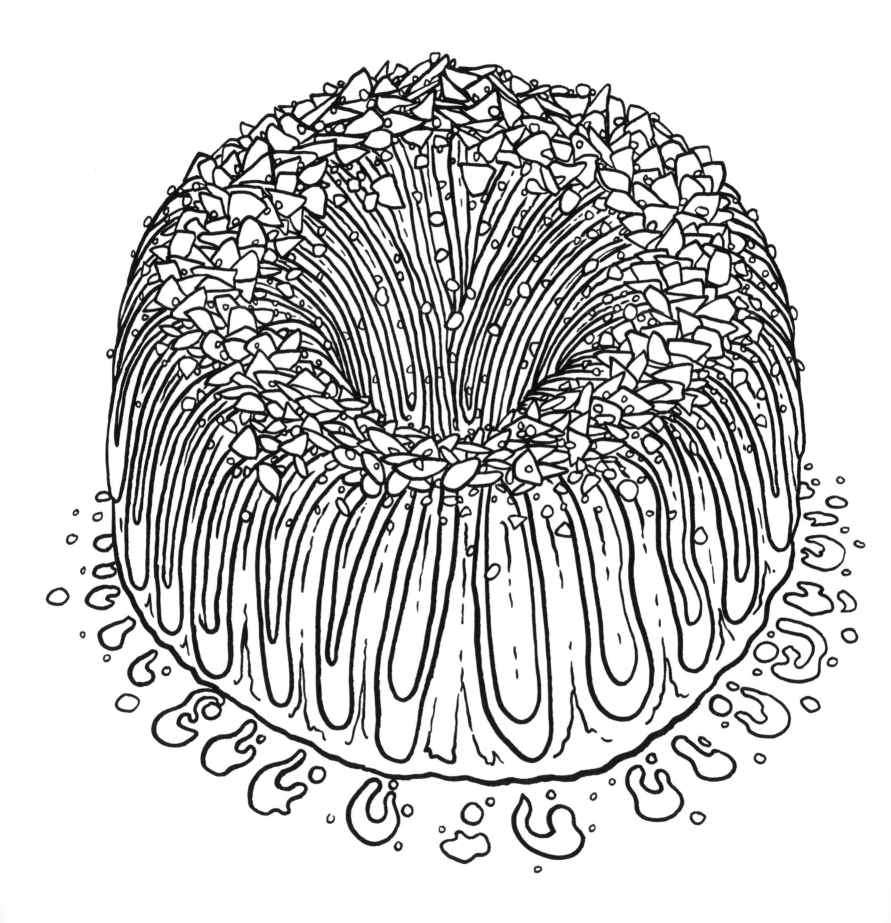

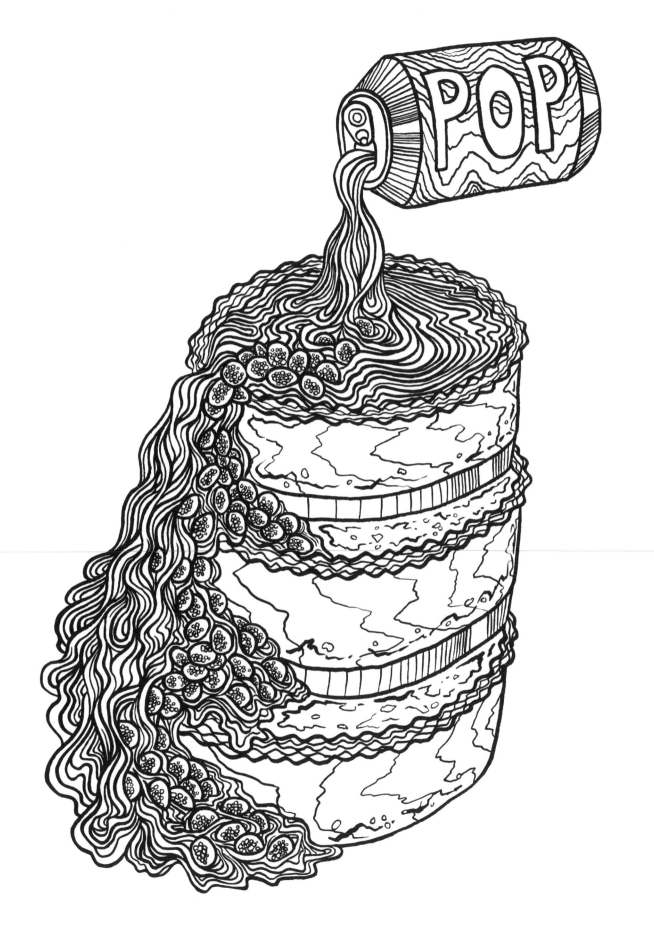

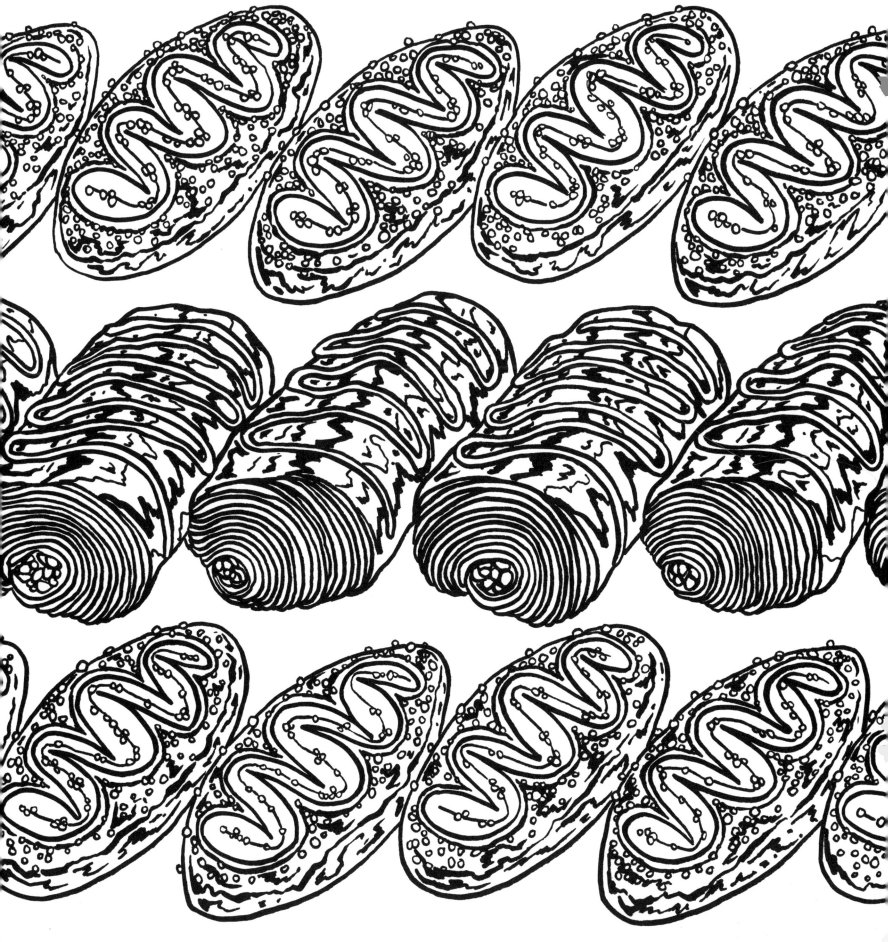

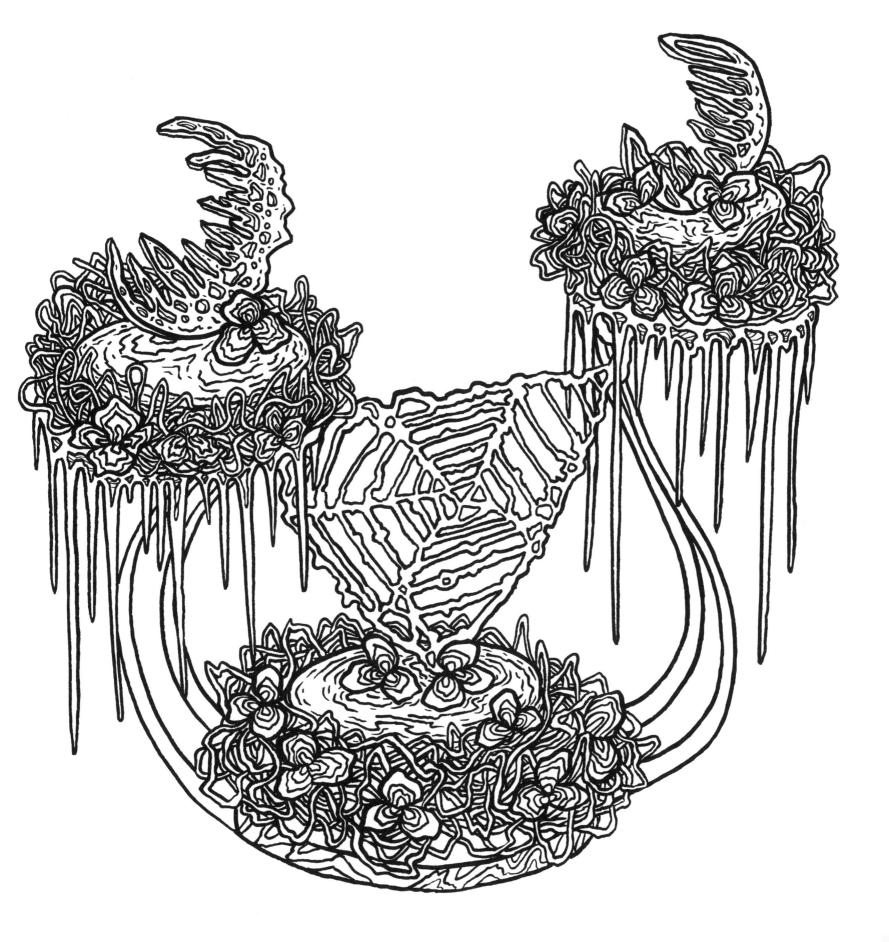

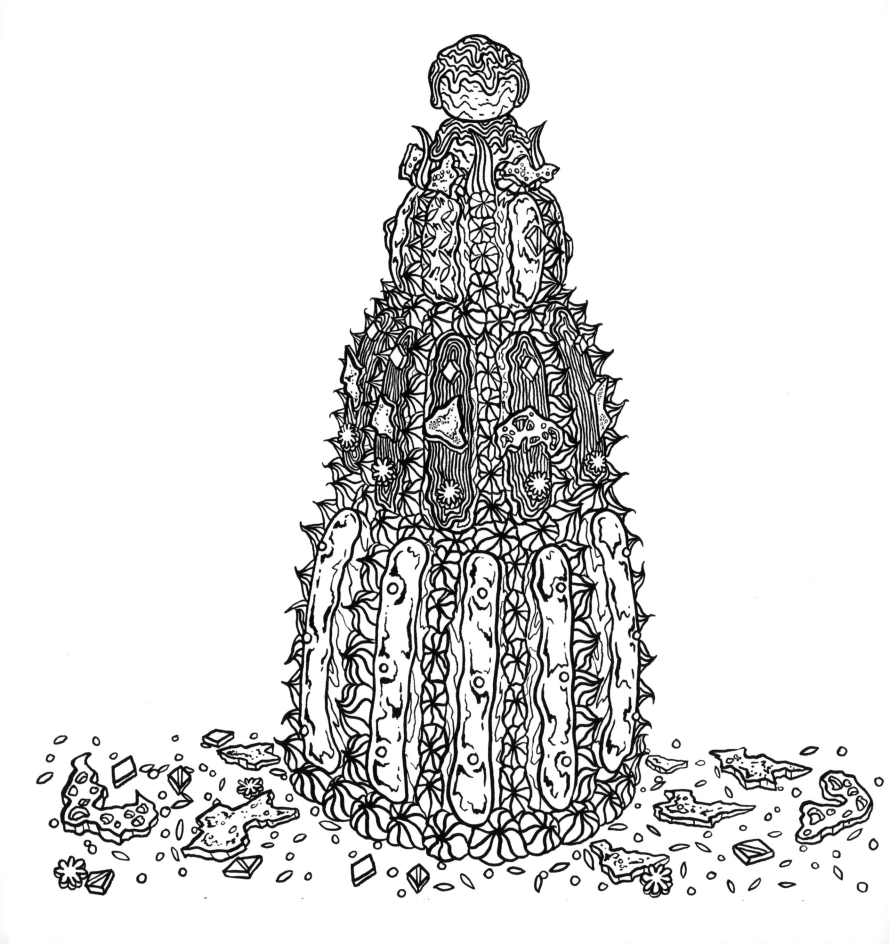

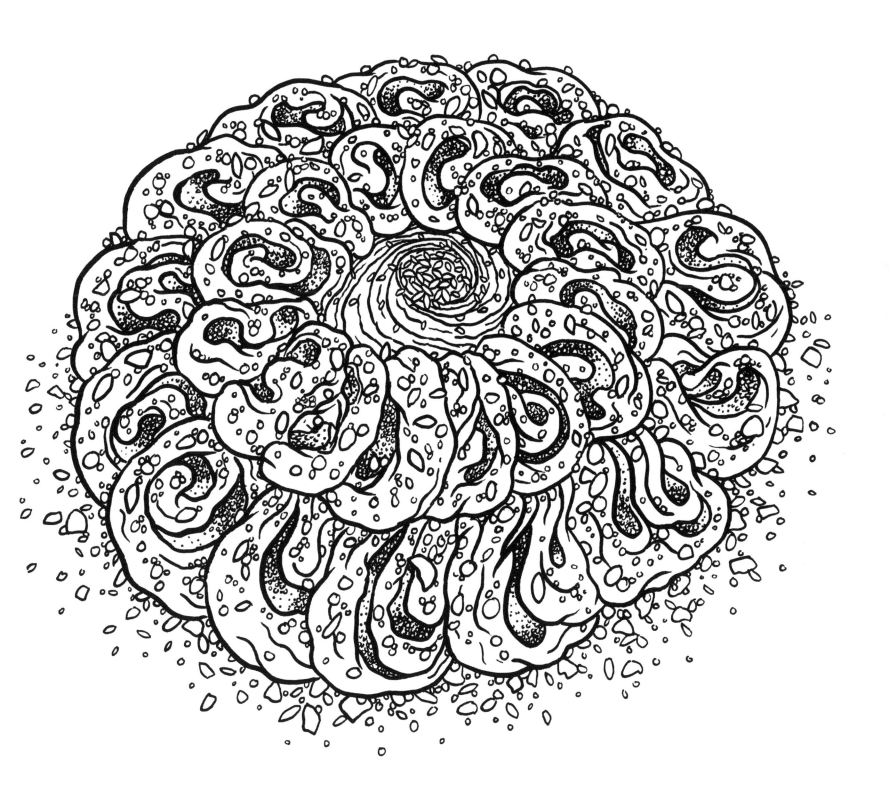

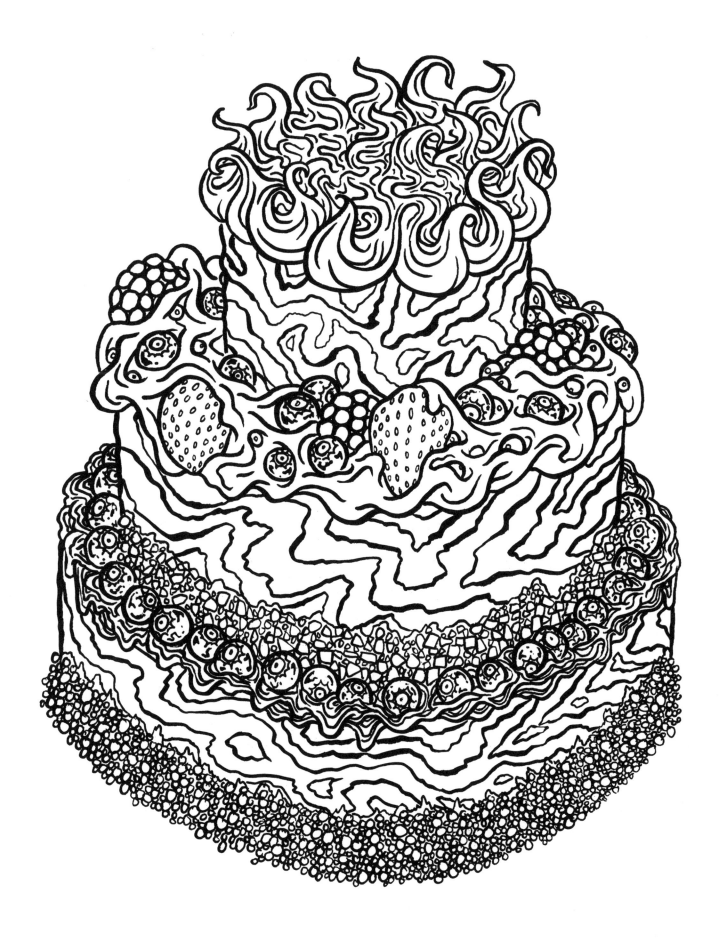

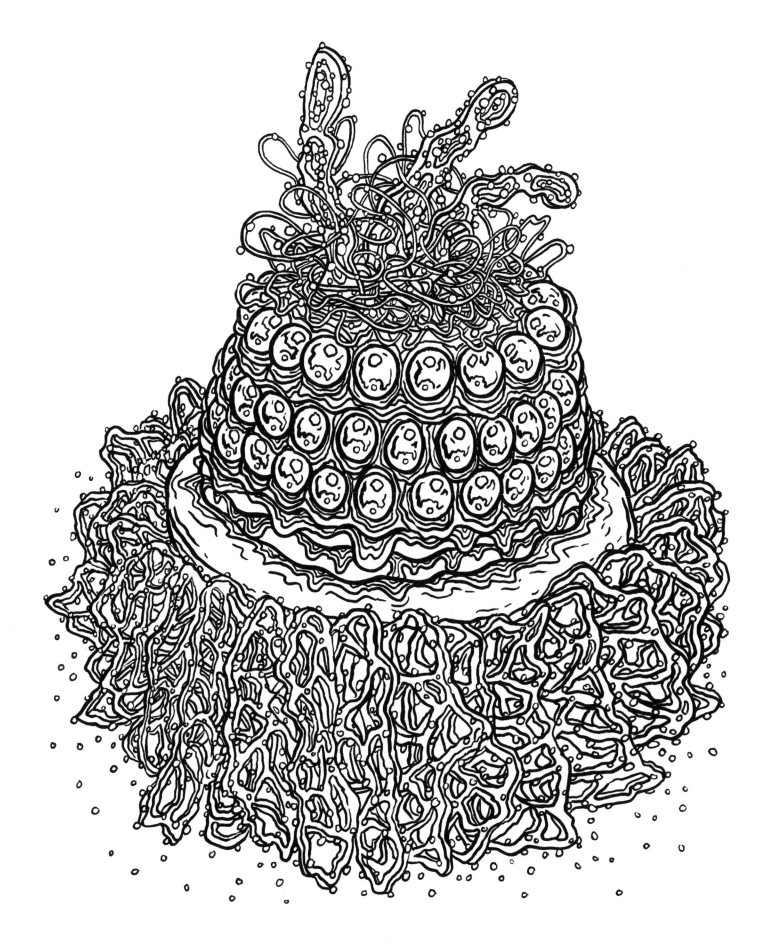

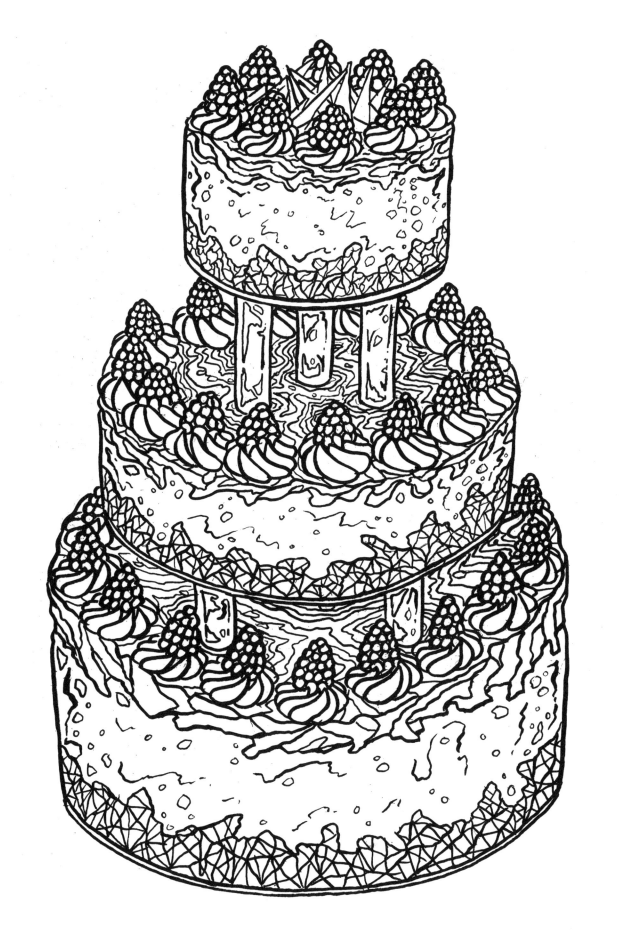

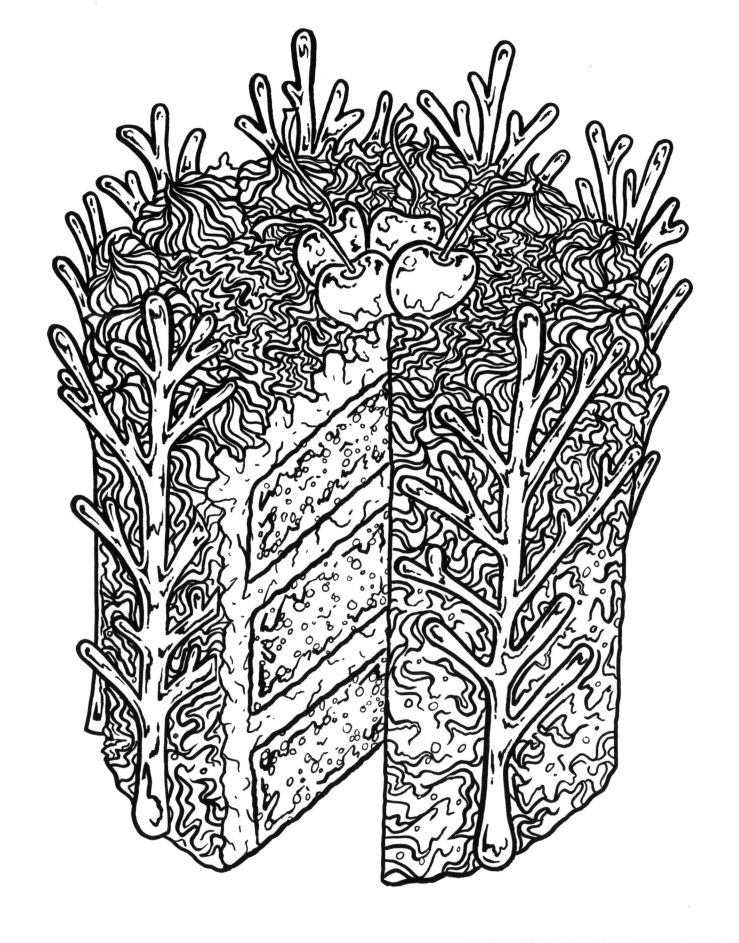

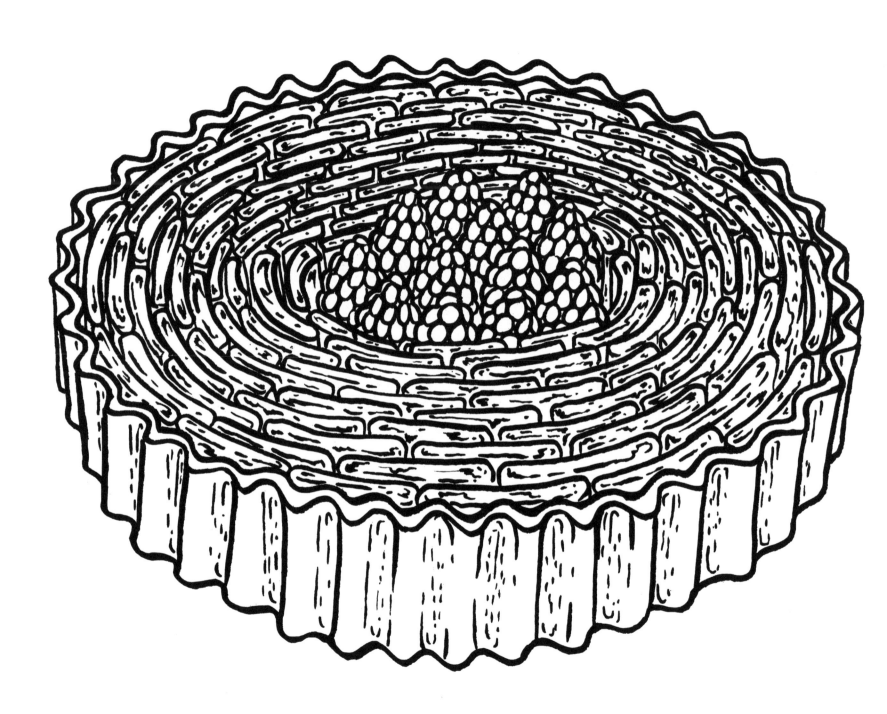

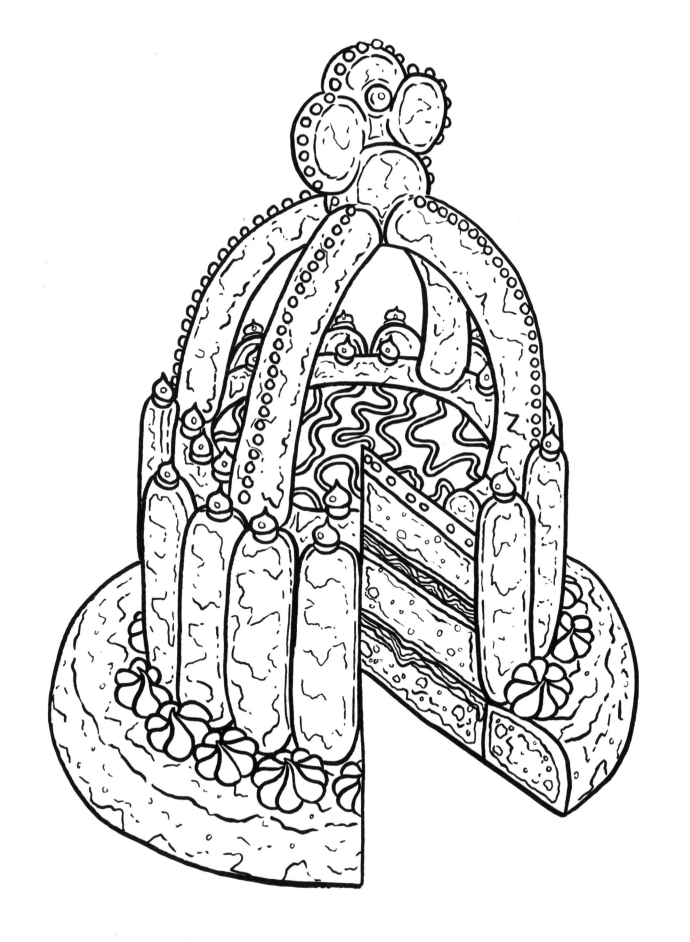

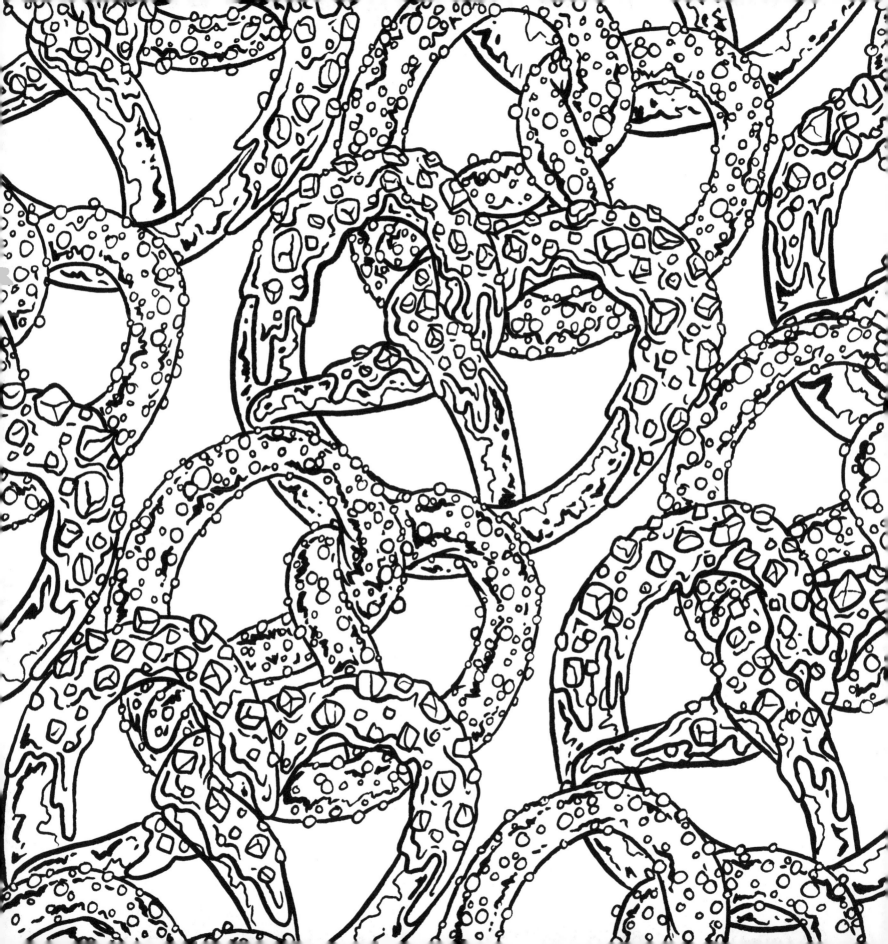

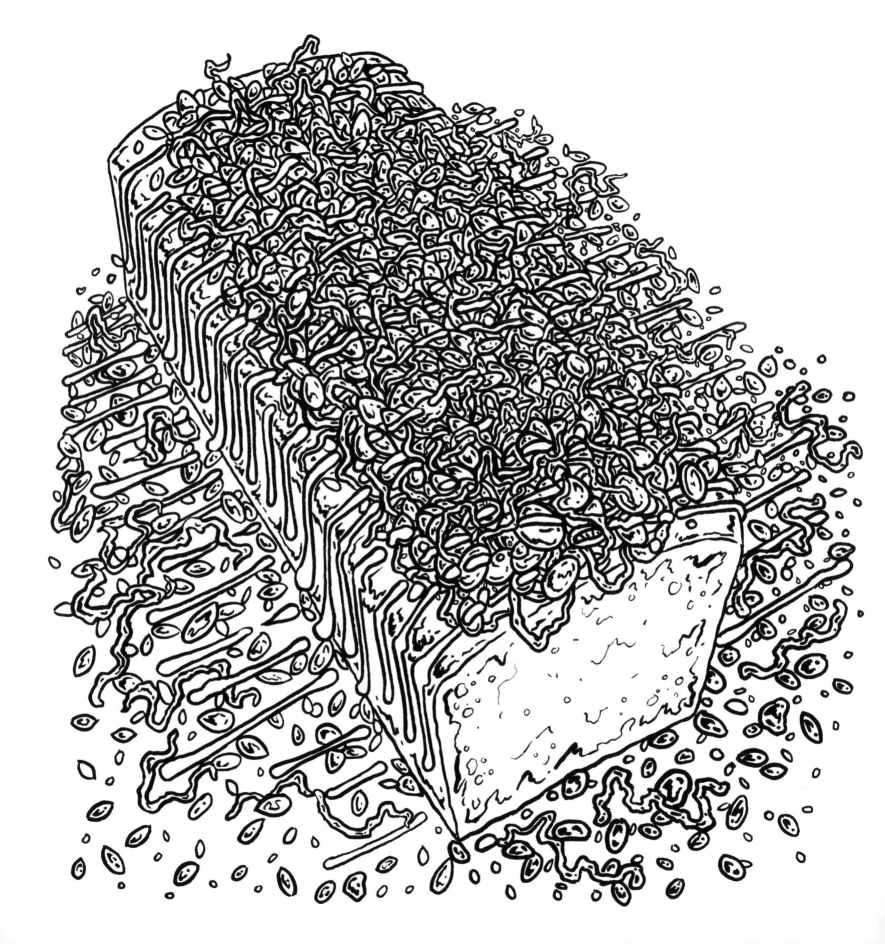

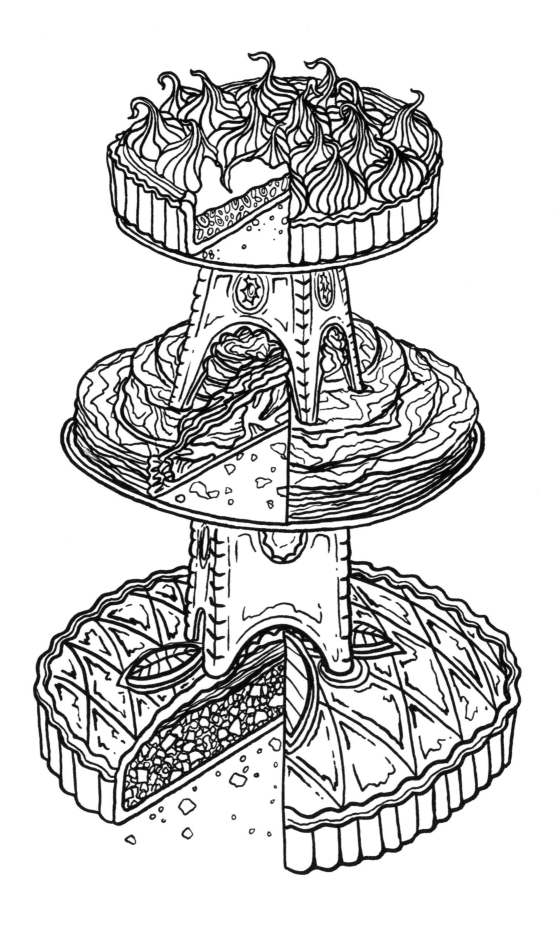

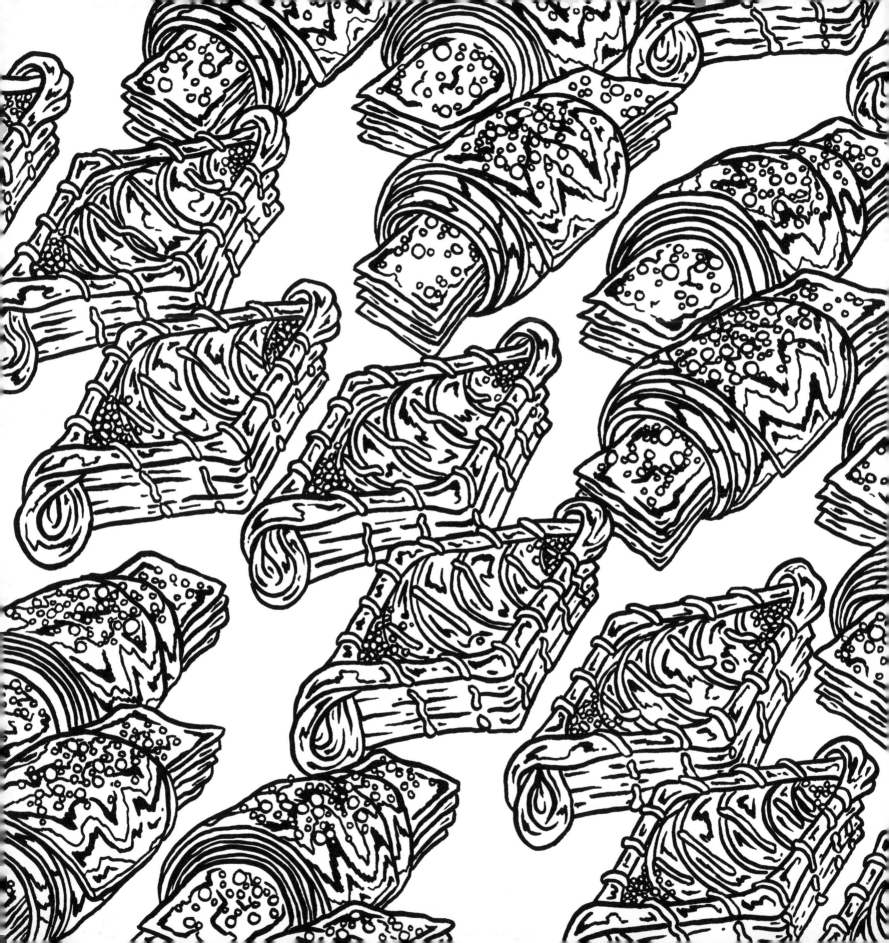

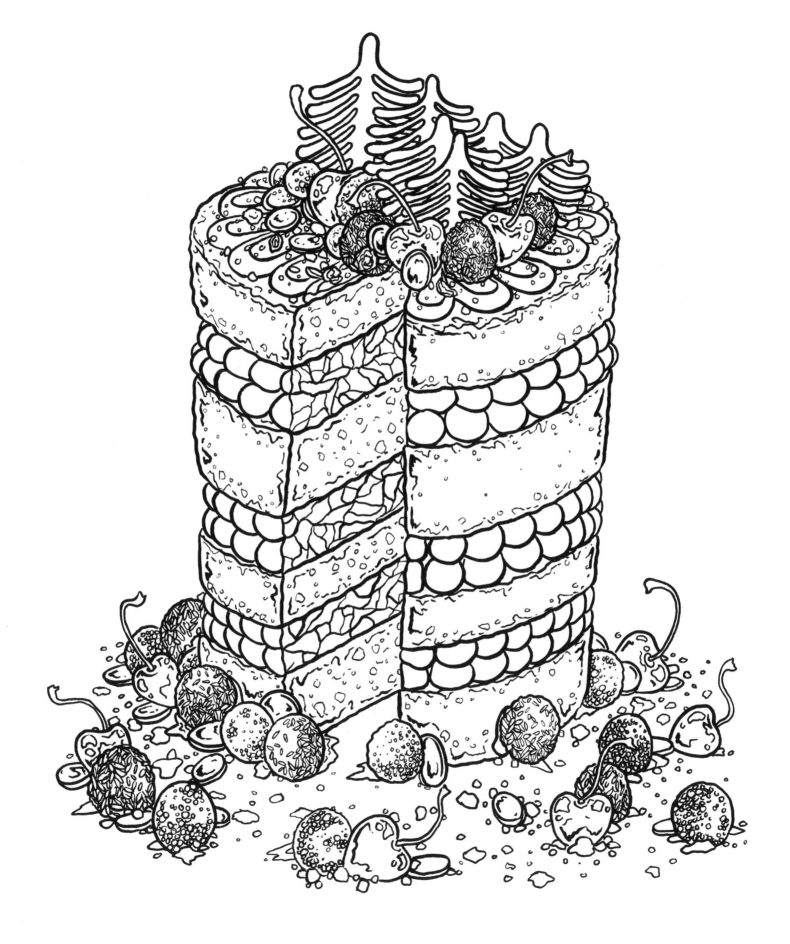

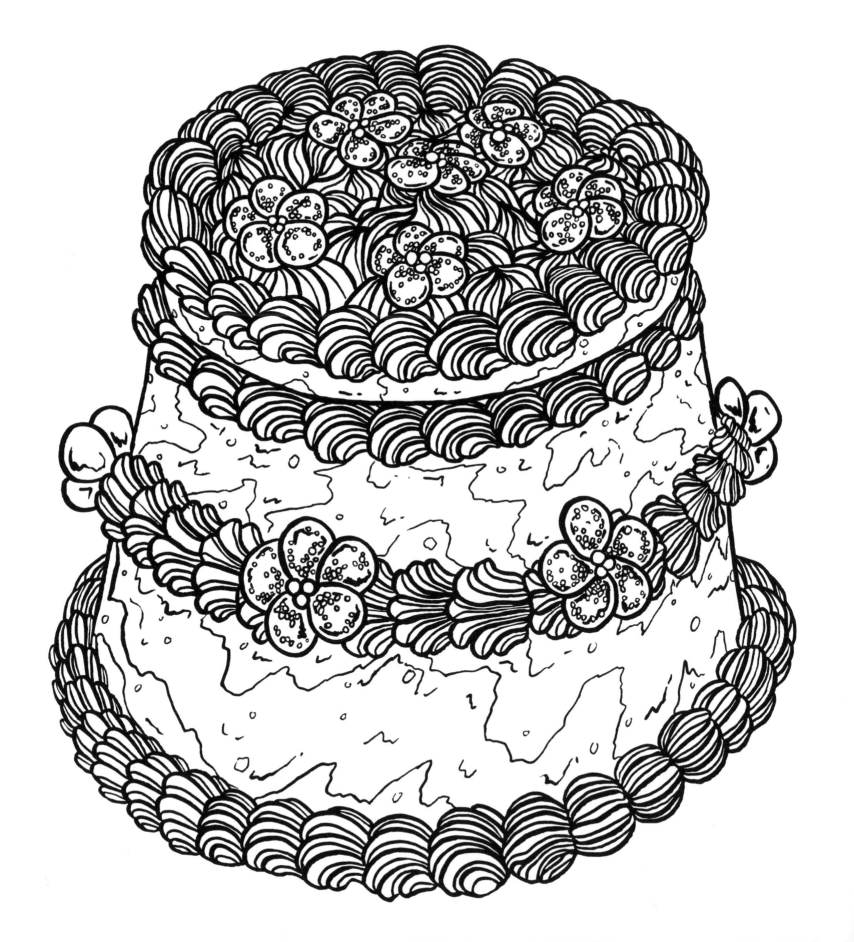

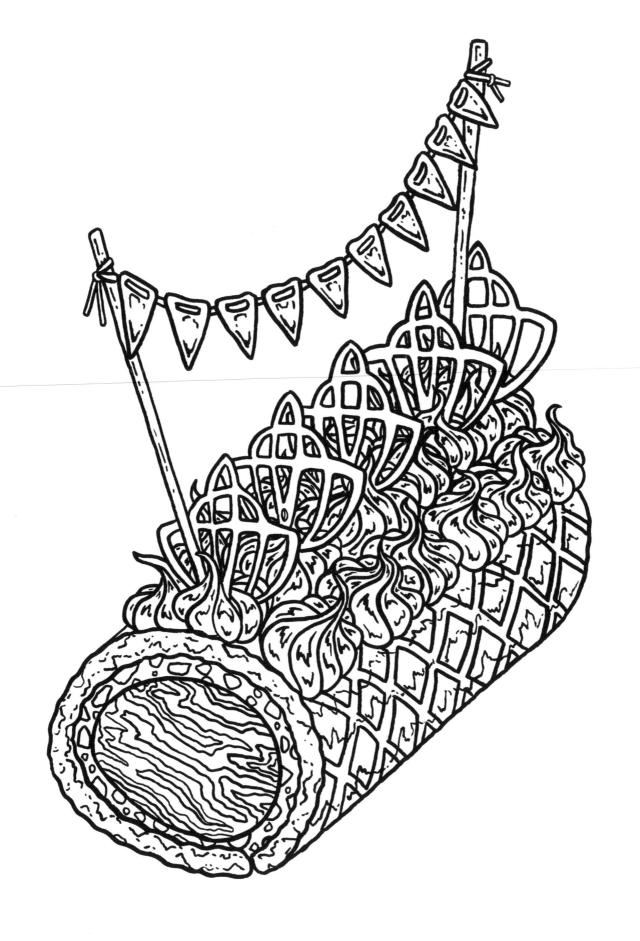

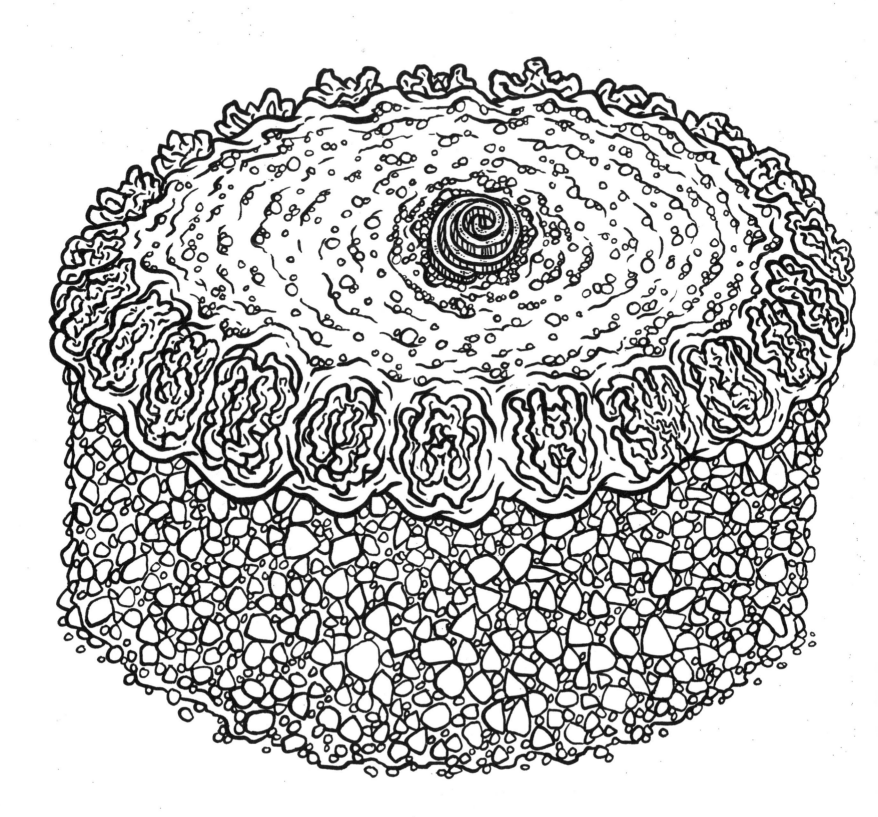

Tamal's Charlotte
Russe, Series 6

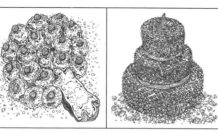

Luis's Fruit Loaf,
Series 5

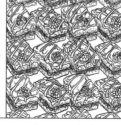

Mat's Tiered
Cheesecakes, Series 6

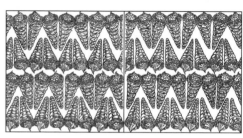

Paul Hollywood's Cream Horns,
Series 6

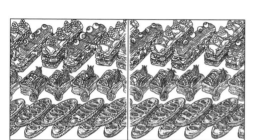

Chetna's Swiss Roll,
Series 5

Paul's Bread Sculpture,
Series 6

Paul Hollywood's
Couronne, Series 4

Ruby's Traybake,
Series 4

 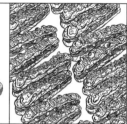

Mary Berry's Opera
Cake, Series 4

Martha's Custard Tart,
Series 5

Christine's Puff Pastry Canapés,
Series 4

Nadiya's Sugar-free
Cake, Series 6

Paul's Povitica,
Series 5

Luis's Éclairs,
Series 5

Kimberley's Biscuit
Tower, Series 4

Nadiya's Ice Cream
Roll, Series 6

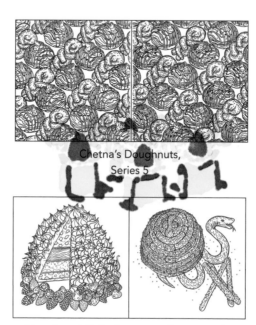

Chetna's Doughnuts,
Series 5

Frances's Puff Pastry
Canapés, Series 4

Tamal's Chocolate
Centrepiece,
Series 6

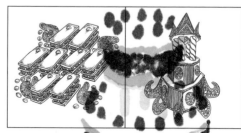

Richard's Filled Loaf,
Series 5

Frances's Chocolate
Cake, Series 4

Mary Berry's Baked
Alaska, Series 5

Nadiya's Bread
Sculpture, Series 6

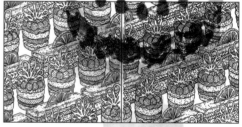

Chetna's Entremets,
Series 5

Paul's Frangipane Tart, Series 6

Luis's Dobos Torte, Series 5

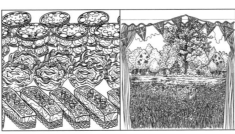

Kimberley's Puff Pastry Canapés, Series 4

Chetna's Tiered Pies, Series 5

Christine's Biscuit Tower, Series 4

Flora's Vol-au-Vents, Series 6

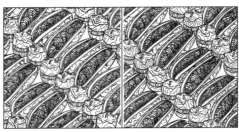

Martha's Yeast-leavened Cake, Series 5

Nadiya's Tiered Cheesecakes, Series 6

Beca's Opera Cake, Series 4

Richard's Viennoiseries, Series 5

Luis's Filled Loaf, Series 5

Tamal's Classic British Cake, Series 6

Nadiya's Cream Buns, Series 6

Paul's Religeuse a l'Ancienne, Series 6

Kimberley's Decorative Loaf, Series 4

Mary Berry's Princess Cake, Series 5

Christine's Traybake, Series 4

Chetna's Swiss Roll, Series 5

Alvin's Tiered Cheesecakes, Series 6

Glenn's Puff Pastry Canapés, Series 4

Chetna's Dobos Torte, Series 5

Mary Berry's Tiered Cheesecakes, Series 6

Flora's Biscuit Box, Series 6

Frances's Wedding Cake Series 4

Luis's Entremets,
Series 5

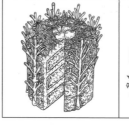

Mat's Black Forest
Gateau, Series 6

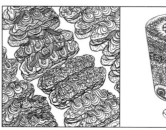

Luis's 3D Biscuit Scene,
Series 5

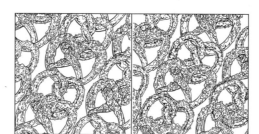

Martha and Kate's
Éclairs, Series 5

Glenn's Trifle, Series 4

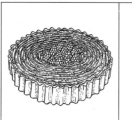

Chetna's Custard Tart,
Series 5

Ian's Charlotte Russe,
Series 6

Paul Hollywood's Pretzels,
Series 4

Flora's Madeira Cake,
Series 6

Nancy's Pièce Montée,
Series 5

Chetna's Self-Saucing
Puddings, Series 5

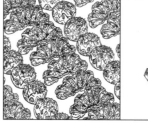

Norman's Tiered Pie,
Series 5

Nadiya's Chocolate
Centrepiece, Series 6

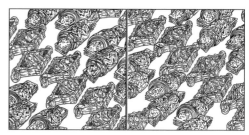

Nancy's Viennoiseries,
Series 5

Frances's Wheat-Free
Loaf, Series 4

Flora's Black Forest
Gateau Series 6

Luis and Richard's
Bread Rolls, series 5

Howard's Biscuit Tower,
Series 4

Mary Berry's Spanische
Windtorte, Series 6

Ruby's Decorative
Loaf, Series 4

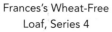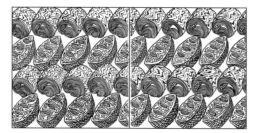

Luis's Viennoiseries,
Series 5

Beca's Decorative
Loaf, Series 4

Tamal's Ice Cream
Roll, Series 6

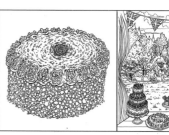

Mat's Sugar-free Cake,
Series 6